When Jesus Comes Again

What the Bible Says

ROLF E. AASENG

AUGSBURG Publishing House • Minneapolis

WHEN JESUS COMES AGAIN
What the Bible Says

Library of Congress Cataloging in Publication Data

Aaseng, Rolf E.
   WHEN JESUS COMES AGAIN.

  1. Second Advent. I. Title.
BT886.A28 1984   236   83-72118
ISBN 0-8066-2062-5 (pbk.)

Contents

Preface

The prospect that the world might be coming to an end arouses panicky fear in many people. But for Christians it is a part of God's good news. For it means the end of all opposition to God and of all the troubles resulting from sin. It means the final, complete, and permanent establishment of God's kingdom. So Christ tells us, "When these things begin to take place, stand up and lift up your heads, because your redemption is drawing near" (Luke 21:28).

This book is an attempt to encourage Christians to look forward to the second coming of Christ as an event that will bring great blessings. It calls attention to what the Bible tells us about this coming—recognizing that much remains hidden from us. Its purpose is to keep Christians from being misled or upset by the many conflicting interpretations of the second advent that can be heard today. Rather, we may await Christ's return in confidence and hope. The assurance that Christ is coming again in glory should be a great encouragement to faithful living in the troubled times that precede the end.

Christ has promised to return. That's good news. Look up in anticipation!

1

It's a Promise

The second coming—the return of Jesus to earth—is referred to in the New Testament more often than almost any other Christian teaching. Someone has calculated that one in every 25 verses refers to this subject. Thus anyone who takes seriously the words of the New Testament can scarcely deny this teaching. Indeed, the frequency of mention indicates that Christ's return was not only a solidly held belief but was considered of great importance to Christians.

This is true not only of the early believers but of Christ himself. For Jesus spoke often of his return. When he was trying to prepare his disciples for the shock of his crucifixion, he assured them that although it was necessary for him to leave them, he would come back. Clearly, he was referring to more than his leaving them in death, for he explained that he was going away in order to prepare a place for them. He assured his followers, "I will come back and take you to be with me, that you also may be where I am" (John 14:3).

One of his most direct statements on the subject came when Jesus was being questioned by the Sanhedrin after his arrest. The high priest put Jesus under oath and asked what he claimed about himself: "I charge you under oath by the living God: Tell us if you are the Christ, the Son of God." Jesus apparently took seriously the authority of the religious leaders to demand a truthful answer, for it is one of the few times he responded to questioning after his arrest. After acknowledging that he was indeed the Christ, Jesus added, "In the future you will see the Son of Man sitting at the right hand of the Mighty One and coming on the clouds of heaven" (Matt. 26:64).

His claim to be the Messiah, given under oath, was paired with an assertion that he would return to earth from the presence of God with the very power and glory of God. The reaction of the religious leaders indicates that they understood his answer as a blasphemous claim to divine identity.

Jesus' assertion that he would return in power and glory was made on another occasion as well, as he responded to a question about the end of the age: "They will see the Son of Man coming on the clouds of the sky, with power and great glory" (Matt. 24:30).

Unexpected

At other times Jesus spoke of the need for his followers to be prepared for his coming. He warned that his return would be "at an hour when you do not expect" —like a thief in the night (Matt. 24:43-44). He declared that his coming would bring judgment on evildoers (Matt. 25:31ff.). To this day Christians regularly affirm, as they recite the Apostles' Creed, that Jesus will indeed return "to judge the living and the dead."

Once Jesus wondered whether there would be any believers left when he returned (Luke 18:8). Another time he commented that it should not concern the disciples if some of their number should still be living when he came (John 21:22). Some of his parables tell of the temporary absence and imminent return of an individual of great importance for whom people should be watchfully waiting—an apparent reference to himself (Matt. 24:45-51). Thus directly and indirectly Jesus repeatedly spoke of his eventual return.

When Jesus left the earth with his visible presence, angels gave the same message, assuring his disciples that they would see him again. "This same Jesus, who has been taken from you into heaven, will come back in the same way you have seen him go into heaven" (Acts 1:11).

The early Christians believed implicitly that Jesus would return to earth. In fact, they looked for him to come in the immediate future, within years at most— surely within their lifetime. Much of the New Testament is written from the point of view of those who believed Jesus would return momentarily.

As the years passed and Jesus had not yet come back, we can see a gradual change in attitude. First, questions began to arise in the minds of believers: Why the delay? Had Jesus been mistaken, or had they misunderstood him? How would this delay affect them? As time went on, the Christians recognized that they had been mistaken about the time of Christ's return. But although they came to accept the fact of a delay, the eventual return of Jesus continued to be asserted by New Testament writers.

Thus Paul spoke of waiting for the appearing of the Lord (Titus 2:13). He listed some of the things that would happen when Jesus returned—even the sequence of some events: Christ would be glorified; he would defeat all his opponents and pass judgment on them; he would raise the dead and make all his followers perfect (1 Corinthians 15). John said, "We know that when he appears, we shall be like him, for we shall see him as he is" (1 John 3:2). James advised, "Be patient, then, brothers, until the Lord's coming" (James 5:7).

The writer of Hebrews assures us that it won't be long until Christ "will appear a second time . . . to bring salvation to those who are waiting for him" (Heb. 9:28). Peter speaks of the glory and unexpectedness of his coming. The book of Revelation gives repeated pictures of the victorious Christ who comes in glory to judge and to rule. All of the New Testament writers certify to the certainty of Christ's return and point out what a great occasion this will be for all believers.

Prophetic previews

Even the Old Testament bears witness to the future return of the Messiah. The prophets promised that God's chosen one would come to carry out God's saving will. Most of these prophecies Christians find fulfilled in the coming of Jesus to live and die among us. But some of the references do not seem to be completely fulfilled in his first coming. There are predictions of judgment which have not really been carried out. There are teachings of a perfect and eternal rule of God, with all people living in peace, which again do not find their fulfillment in the earthly ministry of Jesus. So Christians understand them as referring to the second coming, which is revealed more clearly in the New Testament.

It is doubtful, of course, whether the people who made or heard the promises in Old Testament times realized that their fulfillment would involve more than one period of history. But the promises are there, and those who believe God is faithful still look for them to be completely carried out. These references agree with New Testament teachings as to what will happen when Jesus comes again.

When General Douglas MacArthur was forced to flee the Philippine Islands during World War II, he said, "I shall return." It was a promise he could not fulfill by himself. The people to whom he spoke had no guarantee that his words would ever come true. He made the statement in the belief that the power of the United States would eventually overwhelm the opposing forces and enable him to return in victory. After some years that is what happened, but when he made the promise it was by no means a foregone conclusion.

But since it is Jesus who said, "I shall come again," there need be no doubt as to whether he can and will fulfill the promise. For the one who made this assertion is the one who has been given "all authority in heaven and on earth." He is King of kings and Lord of lords. At the name of Jesus every knee shall bow, "in heaven and on earth and under the earth." When he makes a promise, he has power to fulfill it. His promises never fail. When he says he is coming again, that is more certain than anything else in our future.

If you take seriously the words of the Bible, especially of the New Testament, you cannot dispute its strong contention that Jesus will return.

He is coming again. That's a promise. And for Christians, this is good news.

2

Good News-Bad News

The promise that Christ will come again is intended to be good news. Yet many people react in fear to the suggestion that he will return to this earth. They try not to think about Christ's coming, for they associate it with the end of the world, which to them means complete disaster. At various times in the past many people have become terror-stricken when some great calamity has occurred, because they have supposed that the event signaled the finale for our planet.

Perhaps their alarm is caused not only by the fear that their familiar world will be destroyed, but also by the expectation that they will now have to meet face to face a holy God whose commandments they have not obeyed. The "law written in their hearts" tells them they deserve punishment, and they are afraid that now it will come upon them.

Such a reaction is not strange, because the return of Jesus, which is good news to his followers, will indeed be bad news to others. Whether it will be good or bad for us depends on our relationship with God.

What is the significance of Christ's second coming? It indicates the completion of his work with this world —the final chapter in what God is doing for creation through Christ. It is the conclusion, the bringing to a successful end, of God's saving activity. Rather than being the end of everything, it is the fulfillment of God's plan for creation. Thus the inhabitants of heaven respond to this event by singing, "Now have come the salvation and the power and the kingdom of our God, and the authority of his Christ" (Rev. 12:10). In the return of Christ, his redemptive work—which was essentially carried out in his death and resurrection—is finished.

At the second coming four things are accomplished:
1. Christ puts an end to all opposition to God.
2. God's purpose for us is brought to perfection.
3. God makes all things new.
4. Christ establishes his rule over all.

The end of opposition

Christ puts an end to all opposition to God. When Christ comes again he will come as conqueror, in striking contrast to his first coming as a helpless infant. During our lifetimes we often observe that the forces of evil gain the upper hand and overcome good. The Bible warns us that as the history of the world reaches its end evil may appear to get even stronger. But as the forces opposed to God seem about to annihilate God's followers, Christ will come. He will deliver a crushing blow to the enemies of all that is good, utterly defeating them. From then on there will no longer be any opposition to God or his people.

It is not as though the issue were ever in doubt. The victory has already been won long ago. The first coming of Jesus to earth—in particular his death and resurrection—achieved the victory. The war was won then. But as sometimes happens in earthly wars, the fighting continues for a time, even though the issue has already been decided.

Jesus himself stated this in the plainest terms. When his critics tried to discount his miracles by saying he received his power from the devil, Jesus showed how illogical their argument was. Satan would not be so foolish as to destroy himself, he pointed out. The mighty works of Jesus were direct assaults on Satan and were undermining his power. By his healings, Jesus was freeing people from Satan's chains. (See Luke 13:16.)

This was one of the tasks he came to do: to proclaim release to the captives—and he had done it. In his prayer recorded in John 17, Jesus reported to the Father that he had carried out this and his other tasks: "I have brought you glory on earth by completing the work you gave me to do."

As Jesus pointed out to the Pharisees, he could not do these wonders of freeing Satan's prisoners without first dealing with their captor. This he said he had done; he had entered the house of Satan and tied him up. In proof of that, he released those whom Satan had captured. "When a strong man, fully armed, guards his own house, his possessions are safe. But when someone stronger attacks and overpowers him, he takes away the armor in which the man trusted and divides up the spoils" (Luke 11:21-22). This Jesus did in his first coming to earth.

On another occasion, when his disciples had returned from a preaching mission, Jesus said, "I saw Satan fall like lightning from heaven" (Luke 10:18). This was the result when the disciples proclaimed the kingdom of Christ: it toppled Satan. The Word of God, even when proclaimed by human beings, was powerful enough to defeat Satan, because Christ by his coming had fulfilled the promise of that Word and had overcome all evil.

The defeat of Satan is described symbolically in the book of Revelation in several ways. We are told that Michael the archangel led the forces of heaven against Satan and his angels and conquered them. The victory was decisive: the devil and all his party were cast out of heaven; the war was won. John speaks of this in the past tense — it had already taken place (Rev. 12:7ff.). Again Revelation speaks of a star that has fallen from the sky—the same illustration that Jesus used to describe the defeat of Satan (Rev. 9:1). Later it is said that the dragon, Satan, is bound (Rev. 20:2).

These references all give the same message: Satan has already been decisively defeated by Christ and his followers. The final victory is a foregone conclusion because Jesus has already conquered.

The battle continues
But although the forces of evil have been defeated, they are not totally put out of action. They are bound —restrained—limited in what they can do. But they are permitted to continue the fight against God and his people, even causing much suffering and death. It may

16

be difficult for us to understand why this should be. Perhaps God in his wisdom knows that such opposition is necessary if our faith is to develop and grow. Both Paul and James speak of the blessings that come to us because of tribulation.

At any rate, Satan is permitted, even after his defeat, to fight against God. Although he has been cast out of heaven, he is allowed to carry on his activities on earth for a time. His allies in the spirit world and among people continue their opposition to God, aided by our own human nature which keeps entangling us in sin. God's enemies no doubt fight more bitterly as they realize their time is short, just as an animal will battle more fiercely when it is cornered. They cause all the trouble and suffering they can, hoping that if they cannot destroy God, at least they may be able to overcome some of God's people and drag them down to destruction with themselves (see Rev. 12:17).

Thus the followers of Christ on earth can expect to face severe opposition, trials, and tribulations. This battle between good and evil goes on throughout the entire lifetime of each one of us—and throughout human history. God's people are continually under attack.

But when Christ returns, every battle comes to an end. The war is over. The victory is now complete. "By the splendor of his coming" Christ will finally destroy the "lawless one," Paul says (2 Thess. 2:8-9). No longer is Satan merely bound and limited. His defeat is described in picture language. He is said to be thrown into a lake of fire, from which he can never emerge again. Like a mountain thrown into a sea, which totally disappears, no matter how imposing it once was, the devil has been obliterated as a disturbing force. No longer can he cause any trouble for God or God's people (see Rev. 20:10).

Christ will vanquish all evil forces, including human beings, whether individuals or groups, such as governments or religions or other powers. But his victory is particularly over the spiritual forces that started the rebellion against God and give it superhuman effectiveness. Paul assures us that Jesus will destroy "all dominion, authority, and power" (1 Cor. 15:24), meaning those principalities, powers, world rulers, and spiritual hosts of wickedness against which we struggle (Eph. 6:12). He sums up the completeness of Christ's victory by asserting that even the last enemy, death—which has the final word for every human being—is defeated. When Christ comes, no longer is anyone able to oppose God or trouble his followers.

When things look darkest

This final victory will come when the prospects for God's people appear hopeless. Scriptural descriptions of the last days on earth tell of the increasing power of the wicked. "In fact, everyone who wants to live a godly life in Christ Jesus will be persecuted, while evil men and imposters will go from bad to worse . . ." (2 Tim. 3:12-13). "For then there will be great distress, unequaled from the beginning of the world until now" (Matt. 24:21). But when things look darkest, the victorious Christ will appear on the scene.

The use of the somewhat puzzling terms "Gog and Magog" and "Armageddon" in the book of Revelation (Rev. 16:16; 20:8) may be intended to assure readers of this deliverance in the face of apparently overwhelm-

18

ing evil powers. "Gog" (who is from the land of "Magog") is the name given by Ezekiel in the Old Testament to the leader of nations from all parts of the world who join to fight Israel. The situation appears hopeless for Israel. But the prophet asserts that the overwhelming forces of the enemy will be defeated by God (Ezekiel 38–39).

Megiddo (from which the term "Armaggedon" comes) was the site of great and often tragic battles in the history of Israel. But on at least one occasion it was the place where God suddenly brought victory to Israel when it seemed impossible. During a period of great discouragement, God enabled Deborah to lead Israel to victory over Sisera, who seemed invincible (Judg. 5:19ff.).

These references suggest that as the end nears, the enemies of God will mass their strength for a final onslaught and will appear to be winning the victory. A similar reference in Revelation 13 seems to indicate that false religion will join with evil government to war against God's people. Again it seems the situation is hopeless: "Who is like the beast? Who can make war against him?" But just as God often delivered the Israelites when it seemed all hope was gone, Christ will return to bring final victory when evil seems about to win it all.

Thus for those ranged on the side of evil, Christ's return is surely bad news. It not only means the end of whatever hope they have had of winning the battle against God, but it also means certain punishment for their evil doings. At least some of God's enemies know what is coming and dread it. The evil spirits shrank from Jesus during his life on earth. They knew he had power over them and would eventually destroy them. "Have you come here to torture us before the appointed time?" they complained (Matt. 8:29). This dread is reflected in the alarm of people generally at the thought that the world will end.

Judgment

The coming of Jesus will be a time of accounting, and this is what makes it so fearful. Those who have done evil will no longer be able to escape the consequences of their actions. Now God will assert his authority, and he will hold everyone accountable to strict and impartial standards of justice. God "will give to each person according to what he has done" (Rom. 2:6).

Everything people have done or failed to do during their lives will be examined. Jesus said, "Men will have to give account on the day of judgment for every careless word they have spoken" (Matt. 12:36). Each man's work "will be shown for what it is" (1 Cor. 3:13). Dishonorable actions we may have thought were known to no one or were safely forgotten will be brought to light by the one who "judges men's secrets" (Rom. 2:16) and who will "bring to light what is hidden in darkness" (1 Cor. 4:5).

The day of accounting when Christ returns is spoken of often as a day of judgment. The psalm writer wrote of the day when the Lord will come to judge the earth (Ps. 96:13). Paul told the Athenians that God "has set a day when he will judge the world . . ." (Acts 17:31). At that time "we must all appear before the judgment seat of Christ, that each one may receive what is due him for the things done while in the body" (2 Cor. 5:10).

The idea of a judgment day brings to mind the picture of accused prisoners brought before a court of law. The evidence is produced; it is more than enough to convict. So the verdict is given: guilty! Then the accused are taken away to punishment. "When the Son of man comes in his glory, and all the angels with him, he will sit on his throne in heavenly glory. All the nations will be gathered before him, and he will separate the people one from another as a shepherd separates the sheep from the goats . . . they will go away to eternal punishment, but the righteous to eternal life" (Matt. 25:31-32, 46).

The punishment given the guilty is described as an eternal fire where "there will be weeping and gnashing of teeth" (Matt. 13:42). Paul says, "They will be punished with everlasting destruction and shut out from the presence of the Lord and from the majesty of his power" (2 Thess. 1:9). It's not a comforting prospect for those who realize they are less than perfect.

Many will seek death rather than face God with their guilt (Rev. 9:6). But even death will provide no avenue of escape, for at this time God will call everyone back from death. "A time is coming when all who are in their graves will hear his voice and come out—those who have done good will rise to live, and those who have done evil will rise to be condemned" (John 5:28-29).

It is not strange if Christians, too, shrink from such an occasion. We know we have done enough wrong to convict us. We do not relish the idea of being brought before a bar of justice.

But the judgment that is described is for those who have rejected God. Those "who have not believed the truth" will be condemned, Paul writes (2 Thess. 2:12). This is not something Christians need to fear.

But doesn't the Bible say we must all appear before the judgment seat of God? Doesn't it say we'll be judged according to our deeds? And who among us can claim to have enough good works to outweigh the evil?

The reason why the return of Christ is good news for his followers is that Christ has gone through this judgment for us. The judgment has already taken place. The results are described in two ways. From one point of view, every punishment for sin that we have earned has been imposed on Jesus. "He himself bore our sins in his body on the tree," says Peter (1 Peter 2:24). "Christ redeemed us from the curse of the law by becoming a curse for us" (Gal. 3:13). Thus we have already appeared before the judge; we have been sentenced, and the punishment has been carried out in the person of Christ. Consequently we are now free from further judgment because in Christ we have paid the penalty.

Another way of looking at what Christ has done is to say that he has gone before the judge on our behalf. He is innocent, righteous, perfect. So the judge pronounces the verdict: not guilty. By faith we are united with Christ. So this acquittal is given to us. The judge looks at us, in Christ, as if we had not sinned. One way of defining justification is, "Just as if I'd never sinned." God looks at us and sees Christ. So the verdict is "not guilty."

The result is the same, whatever picture we may use to explain what happens. Because of what Christ has done on our behalf, Christians need not fear the judgment day. In fact it is correct to say that we don't have to appear before the court: Christ has already done this for us. John says, "Whoever believes in him is not condemned, but whoever does not believe stands condemned already" (John 3:18). In other words, the judgment has already been carried out. Jesus said, "Whoever hears my word and believes him who sent me has eternal life and will not be condemned; he has crossed over from death to life" (John 5:24). Jesus "rescues us from the coming wrath," says Paul (1 Thess. 1:10).

The justice of God

The judgment that takes place when Christ returns is for those who have not believed. The picture of the judgment day is to demonstrate the correctness of God's judgment. If there should be any who question God's verdict, who might object that they do not deserve punishment because they are good enough, the evidence is brought before the court. The books in which are recorded the deeds of all people are opened. And they contain more than enough evidence to convict every person who has ever lived. The most arrogant and self-righteous persons will have to admit they are guilty. They will have to agree with the beings in heaven who sing praise to God because God's judgments are just.

The mention of a book in which our deeds are written is symbolic, of course. But those who study human minds tell us that there is a record of all we have ever done—within our own minds. We may have forgotten it, but it is still recorded somewhere in our brain, from which it can be recalled if necessary.

The judgment will apparently vary according to the opportunities each person has had. Jesus said it will be more tolerable for Sodom and Gomorrah—those classic examples from the Old Testament of the depths of evil—than for the cities that had a chance to hear Jesus in person but rejected him. "The one who does not know, and does things deserving punishment will be beaten with few blows. From everyone who has been given much, much will be demanded" (Luke 12:48).

Whatever it is, the judgment of God is right and just. The righteousness of Christ which is given to us is perfect—it calls for no punishment. The lives of those who reject him are full of sin: they deserve punishment. God's verdict is based on solid evidence and no one will be able to question it. "Hallelujah! Salvation and glory and power belong to our God, for true and just are his judgments" (Rev. 19:1-2).

3

Perfect at Last!

God's purpose for us is brought to perfection. At the same time that he is vanquishing all opposition, the returning Christ brings to perfection his work in us. Because he has finally disposed of all evil forces, he can now accomplish his purpose for us without hindrance. Although he had previously done all that is necessary to save us, providing eternal life for everyone by his death and resurrection, yet the continued presence of sin in our human nature and in the world around us has kept us from fulfilling his intentions perfectly. Now that sin and evil have been destroyed, he is able to complete his work. Paul assures the Philippians, "He who began a good work in you will carry it on to completion until the day of Christ Jesus" (Phil. 1:6).

It is in this sense that his coming means our redemption. The writer to Hebrews says, "Christ . . . will appear a second time, not to bear sin, but to bring salvation to those who are waiting for him" (Heb. 9:28). His return completes, or makes perfect, Christ's work of making us new people for his kingdom, restoring us to his original purpose. So he says of his coming, "Stand up and lift up your heads, because your redemption is drawing near" (Luke 21:28).

God's intention

God's intention for us is life. Belief in God as the creator, the source of all life, is basic to Christian faith. Apostolic preaching to Gentile audiences emphasized the idea that God has given us life. The deeper meaning of this life given to us by God is not simply earthly existence, but life eternal—existence forever in God's presence. This is what Jesus was talking about when he said he had come that we may have life, and have it abundantly. This—life with God—was God's intention in creating us.

But because sin entered the world, God's creative intentions were hindered. The ultimate result of sin is death, and death is the undoing — the opposite — of God's intention for us. Jesus came to overcome this reversal and restore God's original purpose. The restoration is finally accomplished in Christ's return. Then death, the final enemy, symbolic of opposition to God and the ultimate hindrance to God's purpose, is finally disposed of. "Death," says Paul, quoting Isaiah, "has been swallowed up in victory" (1 Cor. 15:54). What is mortal is swallowed up by life (2 Cor. 5:4). Death and Hades (the Jewish designation for the place where people go when they die) are destroyed (Rev. 20:14).

26

Now God's original intentions for us can be completed.

Life in the dimensions God intended for us is depicted graphically in Revelation. In contrast to the fate of the unrepentant who have eternal torment marked by weeping and gnashing of teeth, those in Christ's presence will no longer experience any sorrow or crying or pain—because God himself will be with them (Rev. 21:3-4). And being with God is the opposite of death; it is life. The blissful existence intended in God's creation has now come in its completion and perfection.

It is necessary that God's salvation be perfected in us. An incomplete or imperfect redemption is not enough. The most important fact in the future God has in store for us is that we shall be in his presence forever. This is not possible for any person or thing that is tainted by sin. God's holiness is so perfect that it cannot stand the presence of the slightest imperfection. It must react to destroy anything unfit that ventures into his presence. Thus at the giving of the Ten Commandments, the Israelites were warned not to venture too close lest "the Lord break out against them" (Exod. 19:22).

On that occasion and at other times, the presence of God was associated with a cloud. One reason for this may have been to shield the Israelites from direct contact with God, as a cloud shields us from the direct rays of the sun, because exposure to God's holiness would mean death to sinful humans.

But God's intention is that we shall be in his presence, without need of any shield. This means we must be made completely and permanently holy. This is accomplished by Christ in his coming.

Great changes

Obviously this means great changes must take place in us. Paul lists some of them. Rather than being subject to corruption or decay, we shall be imperishable—forever immune to destructive change. Rather than having a nature that may bring dishonor to God, we shall only and always give him glory. Rather than being beset by weakness so we are unable to do his will, we shall have power to serve him as we should. Rather than being limited to the physical, that is, human nature, and thus restricted by the boundaries of flesh, space, and time, we shall be spiritual, capable of boundless growth and achievement. Rather than being mortal, that is, subject to death, we shall be immortal. These are some of the changes Christ will accomplish in us (see 1 Cor. 15:42-54).

The result is that we shall be blameless (1 Cor. 1:8), pure and blameless (Phil. 1:10). Paul tells the Philippians, "We eagerly await a Savior from there, the Lord Jesus Christ, who . . . will transform our lowly bodies so that they will be like his glorious body" (Phil. 3:21). John states it more simply: "We shall be like him" (1 John 3:2). And that means perfect. No wonder Christians await "the blessed hope—the glorious appearing of our great God and Savior, Jesus Christ, who gave himself for us to redeem us from all wickedness and to purify for himself a people that are his very own . . ." (Titus 2:13-14).

Harvest time

An illustration used more than once to describe the end of the world is that of harvest or reaping. Like judgment, this has two meanings. The followers of evil will be reaped — separated from God's people and punished, like chaff that is separated from the grain and burned. "As the weeds are pulled up and burned in the fire, so it will be at the end of the age. The Son of man will send out his angels, and they will weed out of his kingdom everything that causes sin and all who do evil. They will throw them into the fiery furnace . . ." (Matt. 13:40-42).

But for believers the picture of harvest is a positive one. The purpose of God is achieved in us, just as a farmer's purpose is achieved by harvesting grain and putting it into granaries. So the followers of Christ will be gathered into his heavenly "storehouse"—not just as individuals, but in company with all other believers. This fellowship—the communion of saints—is one of the blessings of heaven. We get an imperfect preview of it in this life in the fellowship of the church.

When we are harvested, we shall be brought to the place Christ has prepared for us, where we can continue to do God's will and serve in God's presence forever. This doesn't mean we become God or are absorbed into God. We shall still exist as individuals. Nor will everybody become a carbon copy of everyone else. There will be differences in heaven as on earth. Paul compares the glory of our life with Christ with the glories of heavenly bodies: they differ in the glory they have (1 Cor. 15:38ff.).

In part, the differences depend on our relationship to Christ on earth. The Holy Spirit is working in us now to accomplish God's will. As we respond to the Spirit's work, we are enabled to grow so that we can receive more and more of the Spirit's blessings. This continues into eternal life. Thus the apostles were told they would have thrones in heaven. Whatever that may mean, it indicates that those who have been closest to Christ will receive more blessings.

But there will be no jealousy—no rueful comparison of ourselves with others, as happens so often on earth. In God's kingdom we are all perfect and complete—all that we can be or want to be. Someone has compared the beings in heaven to cups: some are small, some are large. But all are filled to overflowing. Each of us will have all the blessings we are capable of receiving so we are never tempted to compare ourselves with others.

This same Holy Spirit who enables us to receive God's gifts is our assurance of all these good things to come, "the deposit guaranteeing our inheritance until the redemption of those who are God's possession" (Eph. 1:14). And we have the promise that all who believe have this Holy Spirit, who is working in us to make us ready to receive Christ and the perfection he will bring when he comes.

No wonder Christians look forward to the coming of Christ! It means we finally become what God intends.

4

A New Creation

God makes all things new. This achievement in us is not the end result of a process whereby we gradually become better and better until we finally attain perfection. God's purpose is not accomplished by tinkering with the old model, adding some new parts or repairing or replacing what is defective.

What we are when Christ gets us is entirely beyond repair. Paul says we are dead in transgressions and sins (Eph. 2:1). It's too late to make any improvements; we're beyond hope. "Flesh gives birth to flesh," said Jesus (John 3:6)—it can never be anything else. Our human nature is so spoiled by sin that it is incapable of being made worthy of God. All of us, including the most respected, desire the opposite of what God intends for us. We are turned inward on ourselves, seeking to satisfy our own desires rather than love God and care for other people. We are rebels against God and creation.

In order to make us what we were created to be, God must start over with us from the beginning. God must again call on his creative power and give us new life. This alone makes it possible for us to enter God's presence.

Born again

One might say this creation of new life takes place at two times or in two ways. When a person believes, he or she is born anew. The person's old nature, dead in sin, is sloughed off, like the old skin of a reptile. It is replaced by an entirely new creation. We are given a new nature, created by God to live in God's presence. This is the way God sees us, through Christ.

Yet on earth this new nature must coexist with our sinful nature—in the same person. Our old nature, dead and worthless as it is, still hangs onto us. It prevents us from being the perfect being God wants. We are at the same time holy and sinful; we continue to have both natures as long as we live. Although our old nature dies in Christ's death, it has remarkable recuperative powers and re-emerges every day—like the actor who shows up in a new Broadway play the day after he dies in a television series. So Luther says this old nature must be drowned by daily sorrow and repentance and a new person must daily come forth and arise.

The Holy Spirit, to be sure, is at work in us, strengthening our new nature and rooting out the old Adam, that is, our old nature. Christians do grow in faith during their lifetimes as a result of his work. But because they are still linked to their old nature, they never attain

32

perfection. No matter how far we progress, at the end of our life we still have not shaken off our old imperfect self. The new nature we have been given is accepted by God as holy only on the basis of Christ's righteousness.

Then we die—the final proof that sin is still with us. But again the creator works a miracle of life—one might say for a second time, or in another, more complete way. Christ at his coming raises us from death. But what he raises is not the old imperfect being we were. It is not just an improved version of ourselves. That person died. Our weak "flesh" is not rejuvenated. Christ brings into being a new creation. This time it is entirely and completely new, no longer limited by the fact of human weakness.

Again let us emphasize: although the being who is raised can be identified with the person we were, it is not our old self fixed up; it is a new creation. There was not something in us which was good enough to endure. God had to make us new. Undoubtedly there will be some similarities with what we were so we may recognize one another. We will not be merged with God or entirely divested of our identity. The disciples, for example, were able to recognize Christ after his resurrection —though not always. But we will be drastically new. Our earthly tent, says Paul, has been destroyed (2 Cor. 5:1).

Raised

This is the resurrection. It is a central belief in the Christian faith. When Christ returns he will raise the dead. In worship services Christians regularly declare their belief in this teaching when they confess the Apostles' Creed. It is a crucial teaching. For unbelievers, it is bad news, for it means they are going to be called up from death only to go to judgment. But for the followers of Christ it is good news; it is *gospel*. For it means the sinful self we were has been left behind and now our new self can live before God in perfect righteousness and holiness forever. The frustration we have had to live with because our lives are always affected by sin is now forever taken away.

Paul takes pains to show the Corinthians how essential to faith is the belief in the resurrection (1 Cor. 15:12ff.). If there is no resurrection, Christ was not raised, and there is no hope for any of us. If we are not raised we remain in our sins and face condemnation. But the Bible insists on the good news of the resurrection. Christ was raised first. His resurrection is the first installment, the down payment or guarantee assuring us that we too shall be raised. "In Christ all will be made alive" (1 Cor. 15:22).

The resurrection life is entirely new. Everything is new. Revelation says we shall have a new name: a name that identifies us with Christ. It says we shall sing a new song, a song we didn't know before, for now we understand God's grace more fully and are able to express our praise more adequately.

One of the characteristics of God is the ability to make new things and to make old things new. In the resurrection life God has used this ability: all is new.

This does not only apply to people. It includes the whole creation. For the whole created universe labors under the burden of sin, groaning to be relieved. It too shall be set free from its bondage to decay in order to share the glorious liberty of the children of God (Rom. 8:21-22).

This newness means the destruction of the old. Just as our old self died with Christ, so the old world will pass away. "The world in its present form is passing away," says Paul (1 Cor. 7:31). There will be a new heaven and a new earth. Whether it will have any resemblance to the present world we do not know. But it will be a glorious, perfect place. There everything will be as Christ wants it: perfect. Thus we look forward, says Peter, "to a new heaven and a new earth, the home of righteousness" (2 Peter 3:13). Revelation speaks of a place with perfect dimensions, sparkling with jewels—an attempt to describe a perfect place—perfect because God has made it new and because he himself is its center.

5

Christ the Ruler

Christ establishes his rule over all. Over this new and perfect creation Christ rules. This is the goal toward which all history has been moving. This is what the angel promised Mary before the birth of Jesus: "He will reign over the house of Jacob forever; his kingdom will never end" (Luke 1:33). This is what the prophets of old foresaw. In Christ's return is accomplished all that God has always intended for creation.

Paul speaks of it as a mystery. He doesn't mean that it is mysterious in the sense of being eerie or beyond explanation, but simply that most people did not know or understand what God was doing. They couldn't figure it out until they were told. God's intention, Paul says, is that all things, people and universe, shall be united under the eternal lordship of Christ (Eph. 1:9-10). That isn't mysterious, but it obviously has not been

understood by many people. Christ is to be proclaimed
Lord of lords and King of kings. At his coming this
happens. "The kingdom of the world has become the
kingdom of our Lord and of his Christ, and he will reign
for ever and ever" (Rev. 11:15).

He must reign, says Paul, until he has put all his enemies under his feet, that is, until he has completely
subjugated them. Then what? After he has defeated the
opposition, perfected his people, and established his
rule, he will deliver the kingdom to his Father (1 Cor.
15:24-25).

Does this mean Christ no longer rules? Does Christ
rule, or the Father? Both. We distinguish between the
persons of the Trinity in our attempt to understand
God's activity. But remember, God is one. Just as Christ
and the Holy Spirit were involved in the creation, although we usually speak of it as the Father's work, so
the persons of the Godhead are all involved in the
eternal reign over the universe. Christ reigns. He turns
the kingdom over to the Father, and the Father reigns.
God, three in one, reigns.

The statement that Christ hands over the kingdom to
his Father is also a way of saying that his task has been
completed. The assignment given to the Son has been
carried out to perfection. Just as a contractor hands over
the keys for a new building to the owner to symbolize
the completion of construction, so Christ delivers the
kingdom to his Father as a symbol that the work of
redemption is finished.

A king who serves

This kingdom is ruled by a remarkable and unusual
king. For this king says he will come and serve his peo-

ple (Luke 12:37) rather than demanding that they serve him. Of course, that is how Jesus came to earth: not to be served, but to serve. This was so unlike a king that many people didn't recognize Jesus as the promised Messiah.

Jesus is eternally that kind of a savior king: he is always the Savior who came to seek, to save, to serve. He is eternally the Lamb slain for the salvation of his people. Yet at the same time he is King of kings and Lord of lords. The two aspects of his reign go together. For the secret of his glory was precisely his self-sacrifice. The moment of his glory was his death—for this showed his glorious love for us more than any other act could have done.

We shall share his glory and his reign. Jesus told his disciples, "At the renewal of all things, when the Son of man sits on his glorious throne, you who have followed me will also sit on twelve thrones . . ." (Matt. 19:28). The Bible writers agree that this promise of glory applies to all believers: "When Christ, who is your life, appears, then you also will appear with him in glory," says Paul (Col. 3:4). Peter declares, "And when the chief Shepherd appears, you will receive the crown of glory that will never fade away" (1 Peter 5:4). The writer to Timothy says, "If we endure, we will also reign with him. . . . Now there is in store for me the crown of righteousness, which the Lord, the righteous Judge, will award to me on that day—and not only to me, but also to all who have longed for his appearing" (2 Tim. 2:12; 4:8).

What awaits us is beyond description. It is so glorious that it will push from our memory any previous experience. "Our present sufferings are not worth comparing with the glory that will be revealed in us" (Rom. 8:18).

The road to glory

Our road to glory is undoubtedly meant to be similar to Christ's. That is, he was glorified by giving himself for others. That is our glory as well. Although our king says he will serve us, we too shall find our fulfillment in service.

This may suggest what will occupy us in heaven. Of course, we cannot say in any detail what life in heaven will be like. But the pictures given in the Bible indicate that worship—praise of God—is an important feature of heavenly life. The creatures in heaven sing praise to God day and night without ceasing (Rev. 4:8).

Does the thought of an endless church service leave us cold? Then there must be something wrong with the way we worship. True worship cannot be boring. To know that we are in God's presence is always exciting; it will continually draw forth our praise. Thus the inhabitants of heaven are always giving God glory.

How do we give God glory? Not just by singing songs. More significantly by doing God's will: by giving ourselves in service to others, as Christ gave himself for us. Thus others see our good works and give glory to God. This is glorifying God: to help others see his glorious nature.

In heaven we are to be something like angels. We won't turn into angels—they are a separate order of creation, with their unique role to play in God's plan. Created human beings are different and will remain so in heaven, even though they will be changed.

40

Angels are described as ministering spirits, beings who serve the needs of others. In this respect we undoubtedly will be like them. Those who have experienced the blessing of giving themselves for others will not need to be urged to continue to do this in heaven. The nature of such service we cannot describe; it seems unlikely that there will be the kind of needs in heaven that we try to meet for others on earth. But we may be assured that our service will be enjoyable and satisfying. Nor will we tire in our serving, for God will continually renew our strength: we will soar on wings like eagles; we shall run and not grow weary (Isa. 40:31).

These are some of the indications of what will happen when Christ returns. It is not strange that the Bible speaks so much about it. It is a glorious picture of hope. No wonder Christians look forward to the second coming and pray, "Come, Lord Jesus" (Rev. 22:20).

6

When Is "Soon"?

With such glorious expectations, no wonder the early Christians were eagerly looking forward to Christ's return. Paul frequently speaks of waiting for the Lord's return (see Phil. 3:20; 1 Cor. 1:7), and he closes his first letter to the Corinthians with the word *maranatha*—"Come, O Lord!"

Their eagerness is not strange. What is strange is that so few Christians today seem to have their attitude of impatient expectancy. Perhaps this is because such a long time has gone by and nothing has happened. We tend to forget about promises that aren't fulfilled immediately.

Few people today expect that Christ will return soon. Some even doubt that he will come back at all—an attitude that was foreseen by the early Christians. "In the last days scoffers will come . . . saying, 'Where is this "coming" he promised? Ever since our fathers died, everything goes on as it has since the beginning of creation' " (2 Peter 3:3-4).

Can we—should we—live today in constant anticipation that Christ will return soon?

In the first century the Christians looked for Christ's return daily. They were sure it would happen at least within their lifetime. This seemed to be the plain meaning of Jesus' words. Matthew reports him as saying, "Some who are standing here will not taste death before they see the Son of Man coming in his kingdom" (Matt. 16:28). In Revelation he says, "I am coming soon" (Rev. 3:11). Paul argues that people should not get married or involve themselves in any new relationship (such as marriage) which would take their attention away from the task Jesus had left them, because they didn't have much time in which to do this work before he came (1 Cor. 7:25ff.).

But Jesus did not come when they expected him. How can we explain the words which seem to say he would return within a short time? Some have concluded that Jesus was mistaken about the time of his return. Others surmise that he didn't say the words attributed to him. They contend that his followers misunderstood or misquoted him. Perhaps, some say, he was referring not to his return, but to his resurrection or some other aspect of his saving ministry.

Whether the New Testament writers misquoted or misunderstood Jesus is not something that can be proved or disproved. It is really a matter of faith. But let us attempt to find some meaning in these words for our life today.

44

Soon *is God's word*

When Jesus said he would return soon or quickly, he was speaking from God's standpoint. In the perspective of eternity the duration of a few thousand years is insignificant. Compared to the length of eternity these years pass quickly. So Peter says in answer to those who scoffed that Jesus would not return: "But do not forget this one thing, dear friends: With the Lord a day is like a thousand years, and a thousand years are like a day" (2 Peter 3:8).

Perhaps equally significant, Peter suggests that the reason for the delay in Christ's coming is to give people time to repent (2 Peter 3:9). If the meaning of "soon" has been stretched beyond our usual understanding of the term, the reason is to be found in God's mercy. He wants to give all his creatures more opportunities to respond to his grace. Thus he may be said to have delayed the fulfillment of his promises.

It is possible, also, to understand the word "soon" as referring to the suddenness with which Christ will appear. When the time comes, he will be there instantly—and unexpectedly.

Furthermore, time may be thought of as something God has created. Our understanding of time is dependent on the working of our solar system. But God is not confined to our galaxy. God's calendar is not determined by the size of the earth's orbit around the sun or of the speed of its journey through space. God is outside time—beyond it.

This aspect of God's nature—which is really impossible for us time-bound human creatures to understand—may be suggested in the name God gave himself in speaking to Moses: "I am who I am" (Exod. 3:14). In other words God is someone who is always in the present tense. This may also be indicated by the language used in Revelation, where God is called the one who is and who was and who is to come, or the Alpha and the Omega. The passage of time doesn't affect God; with God it is always the present moment. Eternity thus should not be described as endless time, for in the next life there will be no time as we now understand it.

Therefore what may seem to us to be a long time of waiting is in a sense already over as far as God is concerned. There is no before or after with God, no period of waiting. If there is no such thing as time, everything is right now.

Of course, the assertion that Christ will come soon can also be applied to individual lives. This may be the most important truth we are to derive from the use of these words in Scripture. As far as each individual is concerned, the coming of Jesus occurs when that person dies, for at that moment he or she meets God. For every individual this happens "soon"—within years at most.

The delay

Yet it is clear that Christ has not returned within a period of time that we ordinarily would consider "soon." This has resulted in Christians giving less significance to his return—thinking less about it, ceasing to await it. For the early Christians, the delay in Christ's coming caused some peculiar problems.

From Paul's second letter to the Thessalonians it appears that some people, because they expected Jesus to return momentarily, had given up their jobs. Since they were convinced that everything would soon come to an end on earth, why should they continue to spend their time and effort in work that may not have been very satisfying to them? But one result was that since they had nothing to occupy their attention, they were becoming a nuisance to other people. Perhaps they were depending on others who were still working to support them.

Paul has no patience with them. He tells them to get back to work, for no one, he says, knows how soon Christ may return. In fact, he says if any aren't willing to work, let them go hungry.

A similar attitude in regard to the end of the world is not unheard of today. From time to time some group becomes convinced that Christ will return on a certain date. They often dispose of their possessions and leave their occupations and gather on a hilltop to meet him. What happens to them when the date comes and goes and the end doesn't occur?

Another problem reflected in 1 Thessalonians is that people began to worry about what would happen to their friends who died before Jesus returned. Apparently they feared that they would lose out on the blessings of Christ's kingdom. Paul tells them the news of Christ's return is never bad news for believers. They need not grieve over those who have died. He assures them that it makes no difference whether we are alive or dead when Christ comes. He will raise the dead, and all believers, whether living or dead, will receive the same blessings. "We who are still alive, who are left till the coming of the Lord, will certainly not precede those who have fallen asleep" (1 Thess. 4:15).

What happens when we die?

Christians no longer worry that those who have died may miss out on some of God's blessings. But there are other questions about what happens to us when we die that continue to perplex believers. Christians understand that when Christ returns the dead will be raised. Jesus said, "A time is coming and has now come when the dead will hear the voice of the Son of God, and those who hear will live. . . . all who are in their graves will hear his voice and come out . . ." (John 5:25, 28). This will happen, Paul writes, when the Lord himself descends from heaven (1 Thess. 4:16). But what happens to us in the meantime, between the time of our death and our resurrection?

The Bible speaks of this in two ways. One is to compare death with sleep. This is done frequently in the Bible. Jesus said Lazarus and the daughter of Jairus were sleeping, when in fact they had died. Paul uses the same term when he speaks of those who have died. (See Mark 5:39; John 11:11; Acts 7:60; 1 Cor. 15:20.) This would suggest that there is a period following death when we are not conscious of what is going on—as when we are asleep. We are not aware of anything —it is as though we did not exist. When we are asleep, time means nothing; we often awake without realizing time has passed. Thus this period might last for a long time as far as people living on earth are concerned, but it would not affect the person who has died. We are asleep—unconscious—dead—until Christ returns to raise us.

The other way in which the Bible talks about what happens when we die is to say that at death the person in some fashion goes to be with God. This is suggested

48

by the words of Jesus to the thief on the cross: "Today you will be with me in paradise" (Luke 23:43). It is also suggested by the parable of Lazarus and the rich man (Luke 16:19ff.), though we should keep in mind that the purpose of this parable was not to describe life after death. When Jesus referred to Abraham, Isaac, and Jacob to show the Sadducees that there is a resurrection, he implied that these patriarchs had a living relationship with God after their deaths—for God is a God of the living (Mark 12:26-27).

These references imply a transition period in which we are aware and are in Christ's presence, although in an incomplete state. Paul speaks of this condition as being "unclothed" and waiting to be clothed (2 Cor. 5:4). This suggests that we may be without our bodies until the return of Christ when our bodies will be raised in a glorified state and we shall once more be complete beings. Yet Paul regards this in-between state as a good situation: "I desire to depart and be with Christ," he says, "which is better by far" (Phil. 1:23).

These two ways of speaking about our state after death—sleep and an intermediate state—are not necessarily contradictory. As we have seen, Paul seems to support both ways of looking at the matter. If we assume that at death we leave the domain of time, then there is no waiting period. Whatever happens to us at death happens—as far as we are concerned—immediately, even though people living on earth may experience the passing of thousands of years.

Of course it is difficult even to imagine such a condition, for we have no experience in timelessness. But if this idea is correct, then when we die, time ceases and, as far as we are concerned, Christ returns and the resurrection takes place immediately. The biblical pictures of sleep or of being with God are simply ways of explaining the situation in terms that people on earth can understand. The periods are of no duration for those going through them after death.

In any case, it is appropriate and in keeping with biblical language to comfort persons who have lost a loved one by saying that the person has gone to be with Christ. But it is also correct to speak of a state of unconsciousness—actually death—from which Christ will awaken us.

At the same time we should be careful not to deny the reality of death, as though there is something immortal in us that survives death. Although it refers to death as sleep, the Bible is insistent that all human beings die. We aren't just temporarily unconscious. We are dead! It is only the resurrection power of God that enables us to have a future existence of any kind, however we may understand that power to work in us.

Since all of this is outside the experience of living people, we should avoid being too dogmatic about our understanding of it. Christians are content to say that at death they will be in the care of Christ, and that means total security. "For I am convinced that neither death nor life, neither angels nor demons, neither the present nor the future, nor any powers, neither height nor depth, nor anything else in all creation, will be able to separate us from the love of God that is in Christ Jesus our Lord" (Rom. 8:38-39).

No one knows when

But one thing is certain: no one knows or can predict when Christ will return. Jesus said, "No one knows about that day or hour, not even the angels in heaven, nor the Son, but only the Father" (Matt. 24:36). Thus if anyone tries to tell us that Christ will return on a certain date, we can be sure of one thing: it won't be then, for no one knows. Those who claim to know when Christ is coming show themselves to be false prophets, and we need pay no attention to them. The Bible warns us against trying to know the future which God has hidden from us. (See Lev. 19:31; Deut. 18:10-11; James 4:13-15.)

Christ will come when he is least expected—"at an hour you do not expect him" (Matt. 24:44). "The day of the Lord will come like a thief in the night. While people are saying, 'Peace and safety,' destruction will come on them suddenly" (1 Thess. 5:2-3). Since in our day people generally are not expecting Jesus to return, this is the kind of time when he will come.

Christ is coming. From God's point of view it will be soon. For each individual, his advent isn't far off, for it takes place at our death. Thus the Bible urges us to be prepared for Christ's return at any time. But when it will occur in terms of the history of the world, no one knows.

7

Warning Signals

Even though no one is able to calculate the exact time of his coming, Jesus did speak of a number of events or occurrences that would precede his return. These are signals that the end is imminent. They can serve as reminders of his promise to return and help us to be prepared for that great event.

Some confusion has resulted from attempts to interpret his words. On one of the occasions when Jesus spoke about these signs he was answering a double question (Matthew 24). He had made the comment that the temple in Jerusalem would be destroyed. This aroused the curiosity of the disciples, so they asked, "When will this happen, and what will be the sign of your coming and of the end of the age?" No doubt the disciples thought that a catastrophe such as the destruction of the temple would surely not occur before the end of the world. So they combined two questions about these events.

Now we know that the destruction of the temple took place during the lifetime of some of those who asked the questions—and Jesus has so far not returned. So although Jesus was apparently responding to two different questions, the disciples who recorded what he said did not realize two separate occasions were involved. They treated his comments as though they applied to a single event. Thus it is not always clear to which event Jesus is referring.

Yet some of the signs Jesus described clearly relate to his coming. Most of these signs describe trouble of some kind. Conditions on earth will become more difficult, Jesus said, and apparently progressively so as the end nears. Those who look for a heaven on earth do not get support from the words of Jesus. The Bible talks about a new heaven and a new earth, but as far as the present world is concerned, it says trouble and evil will become more and more prevalent, affecting the whole earth, including believers.

Among the signs that Jesus said would precede his coming are: wars and rumors of wars, famines and earthquakes, and disturbances affecting the heavenly bodies.

The trouble with these signs, of course, is that they are so ordinary. Events of this sort are occurring all the time. By giving such signs Jesus may mean to tell us that we can never predict God's future actions in specific detail. We are to be ready at any time, always maintaining a relationship of faith. For it is faith that is the important factor in preparing to meet Christ, not extraordinary signs.

54

Spiritual signs

More significant than the signs in nature and history are those relating to spiritual conditions. False prophets will arise, said Jesus, and some individuals will try to convince people they are the Christ. They may do spectacular deeds—perhaps more impressive than the ordinary signs Jesus gave—and they will lead many astray.

John's epistles refer to the coming of an antichrist. Many people think this refers to an exceedingly powerful person who will come to world power just before the end. That such a person will arise is certainly possible. But John says the antichrist has already come. He defines him as someone who denies that Christ has come (1 John 2:18-22). It is, however, possible that these antichrists, of whom there are many, according to John, may culminate in an individual or power of particular strength.

The Bible warns us that strong evil forces will persecute the Christians. "All men will hate you because of me," Jesus said (Matt. 10:22). "Then you will be handed over to be persecuted and put to death, and you will be hated by all nations because of me" (Matt. 24:9). "For there will be great distress, unequaled from the beginning of the world until now" (Matt. 24:21).

People will make fun of Christians (Jude 18). Jesus said there will be a falling away from faith and "the love of most will grow cold" (Matt. 24:12). Things will get so bad that he wondered at one time whether he will find faith when he returns (Luke 18:8). "There will be terrible times in the last days. People will be lovers of themselves, lovers of money, boastful, proud, abusive, disobedient to their parents, ungrateful, unholy, without love, unforgiving, slanderous, without self-control, brutal, not lovers of the good, treacherous, rash, conceited, lovers of pleasure rather than lovers of God—having a form of godliness but denying its power. . . . In fact, everyone who wants to live a godly life in Christ Jesus will be persecuted, while evil men and imposters will go on from bad to worse, deceiving and being deceived" (2 Tim. 3:1-5, 12-13).

The picture given repeatedly is one of increasing evil and trouble as the end approaches. Those who expect Christ to come and rescue them from the tribulation that will come on this world get no encouragement from the Bible. Jesus offered no bed of roses. "If they persecuted me, they will persecute you also," he warned his followers (John 15:20).

The biblical writers repeat this message. Don't be surprised at persecution, Peter writes, "as though something strange were happening to you" (1 Peter 4:12). Suffering is something Christians can expect. It does not come as a surprise to God, nor is it a reversal of his purposes. He knows that it will come and has allowed for it in his plans.

This is also the message of the book of Revelation. Believers undergoing persecution are given no hope that things will get better. Instead they are told that more are going to die for their faith (Rev. 6:11). Various kinds of persecution are foretold. Evil forces will even be given permission to afflict believers—to conquer, to kill (Rev. 13:7). The only consolation in this message is that all of this is a part of God's plan and that eventually God will win the victory. But in the meantime, it is no easy life; woe to those who live on earth! (Rev. 12:12).

In addition to the large number of signs that involve trouble or suffering, one positive sign is also given. Before the end comes, Jesus said, the gospel will be preached throughout the whole world (Matt. 24:14). This is also suggested in Revelation 11 by the vision of the two witnesses who arise during periods of persecution. They are kept from harm until they have completed their witness. The gospel is preached to the extent God intends. Only then are the witnesses overcome, and even that defeat is temporary. For when Christ returns they are raised to heaven with him (Rev. 11:3-12).

Have the signs been fulfilled?

These are the signs Jesus gave. How are we to interpret them? Have they been fulfilled yet? The answer is yes—to a degree. The gospel has been preached everywhere. Paul wrote to the Colossians that it had been preached to every creature under heaven (Col. 1:23).

Yet even today there are people who do not know the gospel, even though it may have been proclaimed in their country.

What did Jesus mean? Did he mean that every single individual must have been confronted personally with the gospel message? Or did he simply mean it should have been proclaimed in every part of the world? The gospel has been spread throughout the whole earth; but there is no way for us to know if it has been done as thoroughly as God intends.

The same must be said about the other signs. There have been and continue to be wars, earthquakes, and famines. The sun has been obscured by eclipses and volcanic eruptions; meteors of all sizes have fallen to earth.

The forces of evil have often overcome the followers of God. Many false prophets have arisen throughout history, as well as individuals who claim to be Christ. A succession of antichrists has denied that the Messiah has come. Christians have fallen away from their faith.

Does this mean the signs have been fulfilled so the end will come immediately? Or is there more to come? Some interpreters say that since the entire world has not been engulfed in catastrophic disasters, the end cannot be imminent. Yet this is contrary to the constant insistence of Scripture that we should be ready for Christ's return at any time.

The signs have been fulfilled to an extent, probably enough so that the end they foreshadow could come at any time. Yet it is possible that a greater fulfillment is to come. We cannot say for sure. This probably is God's intention; God does not intend that anyone should be able to figure out exactly when Christ will come. The message of these signs for us is that no one knows when the end will come. It could be at any moment. Thus we are to be ready at all times to meet Christ.

The book of Revelation

Perhaps a word should be said about the interpretation of the book of Revelation. To many church people this book is a hopeless puzzle, so they ignore it. Others consider it the agenda, in a code which they have solved, listing the events that will take place at the end of the world. The book's value for us lies between these two extremes.

In approaching the book of Revelation or any other teaching regarding the return of Christ, we need to emphasize again that much remains hidden from us;

58

we should be careful not to insist that we have a complete understanding of the meaning of Bible passages on this matter.

Many popular summaries of the Bible classify Revelation as prophecy, and many people expect it to tell them exactly what will happen in the future, especially at the end of the world. The designation of *prophecy* is somewhat misleading. The popular understanding of the word *prophecy* equates it with prediction. This is not what the Bible means by the term. In the Bible *prophecy* means proclamation. This is what the prophets did: they proclaimed God's will. In this sense Revelation is prophecy.

As they proclaimed the Word of God, prophets often told what would take place in the future. But usually they spoke in general terms, calling attention to what God had promised he would do and warning that punishment would follow disobedience.

Revelation speaks of what will "soon come to pass." But in spite of its frequent detailed pictures, the message of the future is given in somewhat general terms or in symbols, as is often the case in other Scripture. It speaks of troubles to come, of the strength of evil, of the victory of God—as other Bible passages do. It adds some details about how some things will be carried out but usually leaves us wondering when, and does not give us an exact meaning.

It is important to recognize that the book of Revelation was not written to tell readers in the 20th century how the world will end. It was written to encourage Christians in the early church to be faithful by assuring them of God's power in the face of many troubles.

To accomplish this aim, the author of Revelation used a distinct literary style, popular in the first century, but not common among us today. This literature is called *apocalyptic* writing. Apocalypses were written in times of oppression and great difficulty in order to give suffering people hope that would enable them to stick it out. These writings assure those who are being persecuted that good will finally win out. They deal realistically with the evils afflicting the world but hold out the promise that God will intervene to deliver his people when it seems all is lost. God will conquer evil and rule in righteousness.

Apocalyptic literature is not the same as prophecy, although both may deal with what God will do in the future. The prophets told people how they should act; they called on them to repent and change their ways. The apocalyptic writers seem to think it is too late for that. Evil has progressed so far that all that remains is God's judgment. The prophets maintained that God is still the ruler of this world; the apocalypses seem to concede that evil is in control—the situation on earth is beyond hope. The prophets dealt with this world in which we live; the scope of an apocalypse is the whole universe, including heaven and hell.

The book of Revelation is apocalyptic in style. It is written to encourage suffering people to believe that God's purposes will be achieved in spite of the power of evil. It recognizes the troubles Christians are enduring and says they will get worse. But it insists God will intervene at the end of earth's history to bring in God's perfect rule.

Revelation, however, differs in important respects from other apocalyptic writing. Most important, while other apocalypses look forward to a great saving event in the future, John regards this act as already having taken place in Christ's coming, although the final aspects of God's intervention are still to take place. John also differs from other apocalyptic writers by using his own name rather than that of some famous person from history, and by drawing his symbolism almost entirely from Old Testament Scripture.

Like other apocalyptic writing, Revelation is symbolic. One reason for this is to hide the real meaning from possible censors of an oppressing government. Because the life situation of the people for whom the book was written was so different from ours, we may not always be able to figure out the original significance of the symbols used. We should remember that this literature was written first of all for the benefit of people who were living at that time. In fact, we can see references in Revelation to the political siuation in the first century. We are likely to misinterpret the meaning if we try to apply the symbolism to present day situations that have no counterpart in the early church, or try to use the book to give us answers to our questions about the end of the world—questions that may not have been of concern to first-century readers.

Revelation would have had no value for Christians of the early periods of the church's life if its primary meaning had to do with the schedule of events at the end of the world—which would take place only centuries later. Its purpose instead was to enable the readers of that time to endure the troubles they were facing. Revelation can have a similar faith-encouraging value for us if we look for its underlying truths: the sovereignty and power of God in spite of the power of evil, and

the assurance of our final destiny to share God's glory
in his kingdom. At times we may also find that situations
today are similar to those of the first century, and then
we may apply the teaching of this book directly.

Strange beasts, numbers, and colors all have significance in Revelation, as in other apocalyptic writing.
We may not always correctly decipher them. But we
certainly interpret their meaning incorrectly if we interpret them literally rather than symbolically, or look
for their primary meaning in terms of the 20th-century
situation rather than that of the first century.

8

Coming on the Clouds

Jesus used graphic language when he spoke of his return. To the disciples who asked what his coming would be like he said, "They will see the Son of Man coming on the clouds of the sky, with power and great glory" (Matt. 24:30). During his interrogation by the high priest he declared, "In the future you will see the Son of Man seated at the right hand of the Mighty One and coming on the clouds of heaven" (Matt. 26:64).

The book of Revelation uses the same language: "Look, he is coming with the clouds, and every eye will see him" (Rev. 1:7). After the ascension, an angel told the perplexed disciples that Jesus "will come back in the same way as you have seen him go into heaven" (Acts 1:11). What was that way? "A cloud hid him from their sight."

What is the significance of these references to Christ's returning in clouds?

The power of God

In the Old Testament the cloud was an indication of the presence of God. A cloud accompanied the Israelites across the desert, showing them the way, protecting them from Pharaoh's pursuing army, and assuring them that God was with them. When the tabernacle was completed, a cloud covered it, indicating that God had entered it. The same thing occurred later on when the temple was built.

In the New Testament, too, a cloud figures in an important manifestation of God's presence. At the transfiguration a cloud overshadowed the disciples and Jesus, and God's voice spoke from the cloud.

The association of Christ's return with clouds emphasizes his deity. The reaction of the high priest to Jesus' statement shows that he understood the reference in this way. "You have heard the blasphemy," Caiaphas charged.

Why is a cloud used to symbolize God's presence? Perhaps it suggests the impossibility of grasping or describing God adequately. It is like trying to give a simple description that would fit all clouds. References to clouds may also be intended to call attention to God's glorious nature, which is more than human beings can stand. If sinful people should be exposed to God as he is, they would be destroyed by what might be compared to powerful radiation coming from God's holy nature. Thus a cloud is used to diffuse God's splendor and shield people so they may survive in God's presence.

The cloud is also a symbol of power, and that seems to be the main point in relation to Christ's return. God's nature is sometimes spoken of in comparison with the power evident in storm clouds. (See Ps. 18:11-12; 104:3; Job 37:11.) The destructive power of a storm, when clouds are accompanied by wind and lightning, is awesome, far beyond the capability of human technology. This was the kind of cloud that accompanied the giving of the Ten Commandments at Mount Sinai. The demonstration of power on that occasion terrified the Israelites. It is this kind of superhuman power that Christ will have when he returns.

Yet the cloud is also a good omen. For clouds carry rain. The people may have been frightened by clouds, yet they were also aware that life often depended on the rain brought by storm clouds. So clouds were welcome evidence of God's providence as well as judgment. Furthermore, clouds form the backdrop for the rainbow, the sign of God's gracious promise since the time of Noah.

So clouds represent both the providence and judgment of God: God's power to bring blessing and punishment. They remind us of the dual aspect of Christ's activity when he comes again. Thus when Jesus spoke of coming on a cloud, he was referring to the mighty power he will have, both to judge and to save.

But is this statement to be interpreted literally? Will we see him descending from the sky, physically, on clouds?

If there is a physical descent at a particular geographic location, will people on the other side of the globe be able to see it? For the Bible emphasizes that all people will witness his return: "all the nations of the earth" will see him (Matt. 24:30)—every eye (Rev. 1:7). It will be like lightning that is visible far from its source.

The language is probably symbolic. It is an attempt to describe something that is really unimaginable to human beings with their limited experience. It is like the descriptions of heaven. Words are inadequate; all that can be done is to give an impression of something beyond our ability to understand.

No secret

However we are to understand these words, it is clear that the coming of Christ will not be secret; all people will be aware of it, both those who await him and those who dread or deny his appearance. This disposes of the suggestion that has been made by some that Jesus has already come back to the world, but secretly. Whatever the mode of his return, the whole world will know it.

The exact manner—the physical setting—of Christ's return is probably beyond our ability to describe. In any case, it is not the form of his coming that is important, but the fact that he will come, and the consequences of his coming. What we can conclude from the references to clouds, however, is that Christ's coming will be with power and glory such as we have never before witnessed. Paul uses different images, but with the same effect, when he says, "For the Lord himself will come down from heaven, with a loud command, with the voice of the archangel, and with the trumpet call of God" (1 Thess. 4:16). He doesn't mean that God will actually play a trumpet, but that the coming of Christ will attract the attention of all people and will be majestic, as is fitting for the arrival of a great king.

66

This arrival is in dramatic contrast to Christ's first coming, when he entered our world as a helpless baby in an obscure village. Then few people knew about it. If they had known, they would have paid little attention. Next time, however, Christ will come as the conqueror, with all the glory and power of God, and the whole world will know about it. He will come to vanquish evil. He will come as king to receive his kingdom.

The manner of his coming will be such that all people will be compelled to acknowledge: thine is the kingdom and the power and the glory for ever. Amen.

9

One Thousand Years

In the biblical material dealing with the second coming, nothing has aroused as much interest and led to so many varying interpretations as the idea of the millennium. Simply stated, this is the belief that at some time in the future Christ or his followers will rule this world for a period of 1000 years. Two factors distinguish this teaching from the repeated emphasis in the New Testament on the everlasting reign of Christ. Millennialists believe this reign will take place on earth, and that it will come to an end, at least temporarily, when the thousand-year period is over.

The teaching, which takes various forms, is based on a passage in Revelation 20:

"Then I saw an angel coming down out of heaven, having the key to the Abyss and holding in his hand a great chain. He seized the dragon, that ancient serpent, who is the devil, or Satan, and bound him for a thousand years. He threw him into the Abyss, and locked and sealed it over him, to keep him from deceiving the nations any more until the thousand years were ended. After that, he must be set free for a short time.

"I saw thrones on which were seated those who had been given authority to judge. And I saw the souls of those who had been beheaded because of their testimony for Jesus and because of the word of God. They had not worshiped the beast or his image and had not received his mark on their foreheads or their hands. They came to life and reigned with Christ a thousand years. (The rest of the dead did not come to life until the thousand years were ended.) This is the first resurrection. Blessed and holy are those who have part in the first resurrection. The second death has no power over them, but they will be priests of God and of Christ and will reign with him for a thousand years.

"When the thousand years are over, Satan will be released from his prison and will go out to deceive the nations . . ." (Rev. 20:1-8).

Three interpretations of these verses have gained a following among Christians.

1. *Premillennialism* is the belief that Christ will return to earth before *(pre)* the 1000-year period spoken of in this passage. His coming will usher in a millennium during which Christians will rule this world in peace. Before that time, however, the situation in the world will get worse and worse. Only the supernatural intervention of God's Son will change the course of events and bring a period when righteousness will reign. There is a difference of opinion as to whether this period will

come after Christians have gone through tribulation, or whether they will be taken away before the troubles come to the rest of the world.

2. *Postmillennialism,* on the other hand, holds that Jesus will return after *(post)* the 1000-year period in which God's people are in ascendency. If premillennialism is pessimistic about the future of the world before that time, postmillennialism is optimistic. It assumes that the gospel will eventually bring about the conversion of people so that the kingdom of God can be established on earth.

3. *Amillennialism* finds both of these views unacceptable. It says they are based on misunderstandings and insists that there will not be a literal 1000-year period such as they envisage. Some, following the interpretation of St. Augustine, interpret the millennium as representing the entire period of time from Christ's ministry on earth to his return.

The fact that there are only these few references to a millennium in the Bible and that they occur in a book which has the unique characteristics of apocalyptic literature should caution us against insisting that we fully and correctly understand their meaning. We should surely be wary of building a major doctrine on such meager scriptural foundation.

With these cautions in mind, let us see what meaning we can derive from these verses.

In the first place let us remember that we are dealing with apocalyptic literature. This literature is heavily symbolic. All the numbers used in the book of Revelation have symbolic significance. Thus we should expect the reference to 1000 years to have a symbolic meaning too. Although it no doubt is intended to designate a period of time, it would be out of keeping with the character of the book to equate it with 1000 earth years. Not all millennialists, for that matter, hold that the 1000 years must be taken literally.

Since 1000 is the product of 10 times 10 times 10, it has the qualities of 10 to a high degree. Ten in Jewish symbolism represents perfection or completeness. Thus this is a perfect period of time, that is, the length of time necessary for God's purpose to be carried out completely in the way he wants it to be. Since "with the Lord one day is as a thousand years" we have no way of measuring how long this period is.

Attempts to relate the millennium to the year 1000 or 2000 as we measure time are futile and misleading. Even if we should take the 1000 years literally, how do we know when to start counting? Since it is generally recognized that Jesus was born a few years B.C. as we measure time, the year 1000 is actually not the anniversary of any significant occurrence.

Satan is bound

This 1000-year period of time has two features. In the first place, Satan is bound so that he can no longer deceive the nations. But when the period comes to an end, he is released from his bonds and resumes his evil activities for a time. This indicates that the millenium is not to be identified with the end of the world. For at that time, as we have seen, Jesus will come with power and will conquer all God's enemies. He will take care of the devil once and for all. Satan will be cast down, never to rise again. Thus we may tentatively conclude that the millennium refers to a period of time before the return of Christ.

What does it mean that Satan is bound? The book of Revelation on other occasions refers to the power of evil being bound or limited, and then becoming active again. In Chapter 11, two witnesses, apparently representing the church or the followers of Jesus, are said to be protected from every evil for a period of time. No matter what he tries to do, the devil is not able to harm them. When the task of the witnesses is done, however, when they have completed their testimony, the beast is able to slay them—but not before.

Chapter 12 gives another vision in which the setting is heaven rather than earth. But again evil is restricted. The dragon—Satan—is defeated (by an angel as in Chapter 20) and thrown out of heaven. But after that he is permitted to cause trouble on earth. These references may be interpreted to mean that for a certain period of time—long enough for God's purposes to be accomplished—Satan is limited in the damage he can do. But he is not yet totally destroyed.

Jesus too spoke about binding Satan, as we have previously noted. When he was accused of doing miracles, especially casting out demons, by the power of the devil, Jesus said, "No one can enter a strong man's house and carry off his possessions unless he first ties up the strong man" (Mark 3:27). The implication is that by his miracles Jesus has demonstrated that he has already bound, limited, and made ineffective the strong man, Satan.

The meaning of these passages seems to be that the power of Satan is broken or limited by the presence of

Christ, as we saw in an earlier chapter. The devil is not yet totally destroyed. But he is made ineffective for a long enough time to enable the gospel to be proclaimed. People have opportunities to hear and believe, and the devil is not able to do anything about it. Individuals may still reject God's message after they hear it, but Satan cannot stop the proclamation. Only when the work of witnessing has been carried out to the degree God wants is the devil allowed to resume his opposition.

Thus the opponents of Jesus were not able to harm him until he had accomplished what he came to earth to do. On at least one occasion the people were determined to kill Jesus. But "he walked right through the crowd and went on his way" (Luke 4:30). Evil was powerless against him until his hour came.

Later, the enemies of the church were similarly powerless to stop the spread of the gospel. They inflicted cruel persecutions but were unable to prevent the proclamation of the good news of salvation. God limits the power of the devil so that God's own will may be carried out.

This is true not only in relation to Christ's ministry or in terms of the church's mission to the world, but also in personal situations. When the gospel is preached to an individual, Satan's power is curtailed. For the gospel is the "power of God." Satan is not able to interfere until the witness has been made. The witness will not always be accepted; people can choose to reject God's grace. But God's purpose will be carried out. God assures us through Isaiah, "My word . . . will not return to me empty, but will accomplish what I desire and achieve the purpose for which I sent it" (Isa. 55:11).

When Christ comes in Satan must leave. "Resist the devil, and he will flee from you," says James (James 4:7). Christ's power is always greater than the devil's. God makes sure that the task of witnessing to his way of salvation will be carried out until it is completed, however long that may be—symbolically, 1000 years. Only then is the devil again allowed a measure of freedom.

More trouble

Why is Satan permitted to resume his troublemaking after the witness has been completed? This is a question that lies beyond human understanding. Its answer is probably related to the reason why God allows evil to exist in creation at all, and why God permits people to suffer. Apparently it is a part of God's plan of salvation, a necessary factor if faith is to grow. Even though we may not fully understand the reasons why we suffer, Christians continue to trust God, believing that God knows what he is doing. Let us note, however, that the resumed activity of evil is still limited. It will go on for only a brief time before Christ once and for all puts an end to all opposition to God.

As we reflect on what meaning this binding of Satan may have in our world and in our lives, we may observe that this describes something that happens again and again in various locations. There are periods and places when the gospel is proclaimed freely with great results; the devil cannot stop it. The length of time may vary; it goes on until God's purpose is achieved. It may apply to an entire nation, or to a smaller community, or to an individual. When the time is right for someone to hear the gospel, Satan is not able to interfere.

But as time goes on, the forces of evil return to the attack. They are particularly active against those who have received God's Word, hoping to tear them away from God. In some cases the initial enthusiasm for the word of salvation is replaced by complacency, giving the devil new opportunities to do mischief.

Perhaps there may be a culmination of this process as the end of the world draws near. For centuries the gospel has been proclaimed in many parts of the world without hindrance. As the end approaches, the devil knows his time is short, and he works all the harder to do as much damage as he can. In addition, people begin to take the gospel for granted, and Satan's purpose is made easier.

However we may interpret details, the message of the millennium in this respect is that God has limited Satan's ability to interfere with his purposes. As long as the gospel is being proclaimed, whether to an entire nation or to a single individual, evil cannot halt it. But evil still exists, and we must continue to be on guard against it.

The reign of believers

The other feature of the millennium raises more difficult questions. Revelation says that certain people will reign with Christ for 1000 years.

Millennialists assume this will happen on earth. The passage in question, however, does not say where this reign will take place. It seems more likely that John is describing events in heaven.

76

In introducing this matter, the author says he saw thrones. Previously, whenever he has had a vision of thrones, it has been in heaven. He also speaks of the souls of martyrs. In Chapter 6 he saw the souls of those who had been slain under the altar, which seems to be in heaven.

These souls reign with Christ. Where is he? Revelation at times speaks of him in heaven and at other times on earth. But the latter passages describe his final coming when he shall completely destroy all evil. Since evil is to rise again after the millennium, it must take place before his return. Therefore the sphere of this reign would seem to be heaven.

The visions John reports throughout the book alternate between heavenly and earthly settings. The binding of Satan is related to the earth: an angel comes down from heaven to do it, and it affects the situation of nations. If the usual pattern of visions is followed, we might expect the next part of the vision to refer to heaven.

Most important in locating this reign, however, is the insistence of Jesus that his is not an earthly kingdom. When the crowds wanted to make him king he withdrew from them. "My kingdom is not of this world," he told Pilate (John 18:36). When he was asked about the kingdom, as he frequently was, he always answered in a way that excluded application to this world. When James and John, for example, asked for a privileged position in his kingdom, he gave them no hope for power or glory such as they desired. Instead he said they would have to share his suffering (Matt. 20:23). On another occasion when he promised the disciples they would share in his reign, he connected it with a heavenly setting, where "the Son of man sits on his glorious throne" (Matt. 19:28).

It has been a persistent mistake of both Jews and Christians to hope that the Messiah will establish an earthly kingdom, overthrowing rulers and restoring the glory of David's reign. The desire for earthly power and prestige continues to find expression among God's people. But the Scripture is insistent: the kingdom is not of this earth.

Furthermore, as we have seen, predictions of the end of the world throughout the New Testament uniformly speak of increasing difficulty for Christians on earth—not glory or power. Only the return of Christ will deliver them. There is no hint of Christians having authority on earth before Jesus comes back.

Who reigns?

Who are the persons who will reign with Christ? "The souls of those who had been beheaded because of their testimony for Jesus and because of the Word of God. They had not worshiped the beast or his image. . . ." Emphasis is on the martyrs, those who were killed because of their faith, who are said to reign with Christ during this period.

Early Christians seemed to be worried that people who died before Jesus returned would miss some of the blessings that would accompany his coming. Paul dealt with this concern when he wrote his first letter to the Thessalonians. He assured them that believers who had already died would share fully in the benefits of Christ's return. "Brothers, we do not want you to be ignorant

78

about those who have fallen asleep, or to grieve like the rest of men, who have no hope. . . . God will bring with Jesus those who have fallen asleep in him. . . . And the dead in Christ will rise first . . . and so we will be with the Lord forever. Therefore encourage one another with these words" (1 Thess. 4:13-18).

The writer of Revelation was also concerned to give comfort regarding those who had died a martyr's death. They won't lose out, he assures his readers. In fact, they will receive greater blessings. They will enjoy a period of reigning with Christ before the end comes.

Throughout the book of Revelation the author takes pains to emphasize the blessed state of those who have died for their faith. Not only is he giving assurance in regard to friends who have died. He is also encouraging those who may have to face death themselves. "Blessed are the dead who die in the Lord from now on," he says in a climactic statement (Rev. 14:13). In the vision of the millennium he again calls attention to the special blessings that await martyrs, in an effort to strengthen the faith of believers who would have to face great trials.

Some interpret the passage to refer not only to martyrs but to all believers who have died. They consider the phrase "They had not worshiped the beast or his image and had not received his mark on their foreheads or their hands" to refer to believers other than martyrs, rather than being a further description of those who had been killed. If so, "the rest of the dead" who were not raised at this time would then refer only to unbelievers, who are denied some of the privileges that believers receive before the final day.

The question is sometimes raised whether the use of the term *soul* means that these persons have not yet been joined with their resurrected body. It is difficult to say. Bible writers generally do not make as much of a distinction between soul and body as we often do.

Our interpretation of this term depends on what is meant by the "first resurrection" which these persons have experienced. All believers can be said to partake in a resurrection before the return of Christ. We died with Christ and have been raised with him, Paul insists. We were dead and have already been made alive by the power of God.

It is also true that no one who believes in Christ needs to fear the second death of permanent separation from God. Believers do not come to judgment, Jesus said, but have passed from death to life. Furthermore, the Bible describes all believers as priests of God. So what is said here applies in most respects to all believers.

In the light of the type of literature Revelation is, however, and the situation in which the readers were living at that time, it is likely that this passage is intended especially to provide assurance to those facing death, or comfort to those who have lost loved ones. These people, says John, are already sharing the glory of Christ.

Thus, during this period when the gospel is being proclaimed as God wants it to be on earth, these martyrs are already sharing the reign of Christ. This period on earth will come to an end, however, to be followed by a time of renewed activity by the evil one. Then Christ will return to conquer all evil with finality.

Having done this, he will turn over the kingdom to his Father and usher in a new eternal period of glory for all believers.

Passages in Scripture which refer to all believers reigning with Christ are sometimes connected by interpreters to the millennium. But it seems more likely, on the basis of the references we have noted above, that they refer to the new heaven and new earth that will be established upon Christ's return.

We don't know it all

Why does the millennium create so much interest? Perhaps for one thing because so little is said about it in the Bible. There is room for speculation. This is a human tendency: when we don't have full information, we try to fill in the details ourselves by adding what we think is reasonable. Unfortunately, when we try to explain to our human satisfaction details of spiritual matters for which we do not have full information, the possibility of error is high.

Furthermore, the teaching of an earthly reign by Christians is appealing. It continues the expectations of the Jews that made them reject Jesus. It satisfies our natural desire to reap rewards for our faith. Even the disciples expressed concern about this. We want to be assured that we have made the right choice—that we'll end up on top, that we'll be rewarded. Particularly when things seem to be going badly for us, we want the assurance that everything will eventually work out for our good. Too often we seek this assurance in terms of the values of this world. The Apocalypse seeks to give the assurance we want, but always in terms of God's heaven, not this world.

We do not pretend to be able to solve all the questions related to the concept of the millennium. Christians will continue to differ in their interpretation of the reference to the first resurrection. We may continue to puzzle over the interruption of Christ's reign by Satan's renewed activity. We may question whether it is consistent with Scripture to say some Christians will be given special consideration or treatment.

Nevertheless, the reference to the millennium can be helpful for our faith. It assures us that Satan is not able to stop the proclamation of the gospel. God's Word will accomplish his purpose. It warns us at the same time to watch and pray because evil is still strong in our world. And it assures us that those who have suffered for their faith will be the first to share the glory of Christ's rule.

The rapture

Another widely discussed teaching in regard to Christ's coming is the rapture. This is the belief that, at Christ's return, all believers will be physically lifted up into the air to meet Christ. The teaching is based on 1 Thessalonians 4:16-17: "And the dead in Christ will rise first. After that, we who are still alive and are left will be caught up with them in the clouds to meet the Lord in the air. And so we will be with the Lord forever."

This statement, it should be noted, comes in a passage in which Paul is explaining to his readers that they do not need to worry about people who have died. They will not lose out on the blessings of Christ's return. In fact, he says, they will be raised first. Then those of us who are still living will join them to meet Christ.

A literal interpretation of this passage raises the same problems as a literal interpretation of the statement that Christ is coming on clouds. Where and how can people from all over a spherical world be gathered to meet a Christ whose advent will be seen by all? The passage assures us that we shall be united with Christ. The physical details of this meeting are beyond our understanding at this time.

Some other ideas have become associated with the idea of "the rapture." Some think that believers will be taken away suddenly, mysteriously, to be united with Christ. They base this belief on Luke 17:34-35, "I tell you, on that night two people will be in one bed; one will be taken and the other left. Two women will be grinding together; one will be taken and the other left."

But the idea that Christians will suddenly disappear to meet Christ contradicts the plain teaching of the Bible that when Jesus comes again everybody will know it. It won't be secret. When the believers are taken to heaven, all the world will know it. This is emphasized in this very passage in Luke 17: "For the Son of Man in his day will be like the lightning, which flashes and lights up the sky from one end to the other" (v. 24).

Furthermore, the passage in Luke does not refer to people being taken to glory, but just the opposite. Those who are taken are being taken to judgment. Jesus was talking about the people in Noah's day and in the days of Sodom, people who were evil but were not expecting any trouble. Suddenly they were taken away in judgment. That it is judgment and not blessing is also indicated by the conclusion of the passage. The disciples ask where these people will be taken. Jesus replies,

"Where there is a dead body, there the vultures will gather." This speaks of destruction: birds of prey will feast on the bodies that have been taken.

The point of Jesus' statements is that judgment comes individually. It doesn't make any difference who you have been associated with or what you were doing. If you yourself have rejected Christ, judgment comes to you—and when you least expect it.

Some also hold that in the rapture, believers will be taken away from the tribulation that will afflict the earth and that only unbelievers will be left here to suffer. This idea developed rather recently in church history. It has led some to conclude that there are two future comings of Christ. First he will come to rescue believers from tribulation. Then after a period of difficulty for the people who are left, he will come to judge the world.

The language of the Bible does not support the idea of two returns separated in time, but rather indicates that all the effects of Christ's coming take place at his single return. Nor does the Bible give encouragement to the hope that Christians will escape the trouble or persecution that is forecast. The time of persecution may be shortened for the sake of believers (Matt. 24:22), but they clearly will suffer. On the contrary, the warning is given repeatedly that Christians along with others will suffer the increasing tribulation on earth that will become greater until Christ finally comes.

The Christian hope is not to avoid tribulation, but to be united with Christ when he comes to conquer and rule. The wrath of God will then be visited on unbelievers as punishment. Believers will not be affected by that punishment, but nowhere are we encouraged to believe we shall be spared suffering before that time.

The Bible tells of no secret coming of Christ. On the contrary, all the universe will know and acknowledge Christ when he arrives. Nor does Scripture encourage us to hope we shall escape tribulation. We may be protected from some trouble; the period of trial may be limited. But the evils of the world will grow worse. The promise is not that we shall escape tribulation, but that Christ has overcome it.

That Christ will gather his own to himself is a firm promise. In what way this may take place we cannot say.

10

Be Prepared

If we believe that Jesus is coming again, and if we recognize that his return could occur at any moment, it is fitting that we should make preparations to meet him. Jesus told several parables that emphasize the importance of being ready for his return. Repeatedly the Bible urges us to be ready for his coming.

"Be on guard! Be alert! You do not know when that time will come" (Mark 13:33). "Be dressed and ready for service and keep your lamps burning, be like men waiting for their master to return from a wedding banquet, so that when he comes and knocks they can immediately open the door for him. It will be good for those servants whose master finds them watching when he comes" (Luke 12:35-37). Paul adds that because we are children of light, we should not be caught by surprise (1 Thess. 5:4).

How can we best carry out this advice?

Christians who want to be ready for the Lord's return will have an attitude of eager expectation. They anticipate meeting Jesus soon, whether that means he will return during their lifetime or that they will enter his presence at their death. They look forward to that moment as the fulfillment of their salvation. This anticipation of completed salvation governs their days. They live in hope, eagerly waiting for the return of their Lord.

Thus they are always ready to leave this existence. They are like the Israelites who ate the Passover while standing, dressed to travel, so they would be ready to leave Egypt as soon as the word was given. "I desire to depart and be with Christ" is how Paul expresses this attitude (Phil. 1:23).

As they wait, Christians are willing to endure patiently whatever may come to them in life. "Be patient . . . until the Lord's coming," James wrote (James 5:7). Even in suffering Christians find it possible to rejoice because of their confidence in God's loving power which will one day soon bring blessing. Paul said, "I consider that our present sufferings are not worth comparing with the glory that will be revealed in us" (Rom. 8:18).

Active waiting

But it is not an inactive waiting. We have noted earlier that some people, convinced—in spite of biblical teaching—that they know when Christ will return, prepare for it by leaving jobs, homes, and possessions. Often they gather on a hilltop with others who share their belief, perhaps so they will have an unrestricted view and may be the first to greet Jesus when he comes in the clouds.

Paul warned against this kind of preparation in which people stop all their activity and just wait. As we have seen, some of the members of the church at Thessalonica were doing just that. They were becoming a nuisance to others and possibly even harming their own faith by idleness. Paul tells them to get back to work.

Preparing to receive Christ involves action, not idleness, as well as attitudes. As they await their meeting with Christ, Christians make use of every opportunity to improve their preparedness. First of all is the maintenance of a relationship of faith in Jesus.

For this Christians will make steady use of the resources he has left us. Recognizing how important it is that Christ's words abide in us (John 15:7), they will read and study the Word of God as we have it in the Bible. Paul thus advises Timothy to "continue in what you have learned," referring to "the holy Scriptures, which are able to make you wise for salvation through faith in Christ Jesus." He points out that the Scriptures can not only instruct us for salvation but are "profitable for teaching, for rebuking, correcting and training in righteousness, so that the man of God may be thoroughly equipped for every good work" (2 Tim. 3:14-17). To be kept "blameless at the coming of our Lord Jesus Christ" is the goal of all Christians (1 Thess. 5:23). So Paul urges all Christians to "let the word of Christ dwell in you richly . . ." (Col. 3:16).

This is not to be done in isolation. The Word is shared and studied together. Paul goes on in his letter to the Colossians: "Let the word of Christ dwell in you richly as you teach and admonish one another with all wisdom, and as you sing psalms, hymns and spiritual songs with gratitude in your hearts to God."

An important part of Christian preparedness thus is worship with other believers. Worship is declaring our faith in the presence of others. It is a vital ingredient for continuing in faith. The writer to the Hebrews relates it specifically to our preparation for Christ's return: "Let us hold unswervingly to the hope we profess, for he who promised is faithful. And let us consider how we may spur one another on toward love and good deeds. Let us not give up meeting together, as some are in the habit of doing, but let us encourage one another—and all the more as you see the Day approaching" (Heb. 10:23-25).

Worship also includes participation in the Lord's Supper. Not only is this helpful in maintaining and strengthening our faith, but by this act we "proclaim the Lord's death until he comes" (1 Cor. 11:26). In the Lord's Supper we express our faith that Jesus will return and are strengthened to await him in faith.

An essential part of the Christian's preparation is prayer. The instruction comes often: watch and pray. As Jesus concluded his comments about his return he said, "Be always on the watch, and pray that you may be able to escape all that is about to happen, and that you may be able to stand before the Son of Man" (Luke 21:36). Being forewarned of the trials we may have to face, Christians can pray specifically for the endurance they need and thus find strength to stand.

Strengthening faith

As they act positively in ways that strengthen faith, Christians also act against sin and imperfection. "Be careful, or your hearts will be weighed down with dissipation, drunkenness and the anxieties of life, and that day will close on you unexpectedly like a trap," Jesus warned (Luke 21:34). Peter used the words *clear minded* and *self-controlled* to characterize the life of a person who knows the end is at hand. "Since everything will be destroyed in this way," he writes, "what kind of people ought you to be? You ought to live holy and godly lives as you look forward to the day of God and speed its coming" (2 Peter 3:11-12).

Paul declares that God's grace "teaches us to say 'No' to ungodliness and worldly passions, and to live self-controlled, upright and godly lives in this present age, while we wait for the blessed hope—the glorious appearing of our great God and Savior, Jesus Christ . . ." (Titus 2:12-13). John adds, "Everyone who has this hope in him purifies himself, just as he is pure" (1 John 3:3). Paul prays that his readers may abound more and more in love, "in knowledge and depth of insight, so that you may be able to discern what is best and may be pure and blameless until the day of Christ, filled with the fruits of righteousness that come through Jesus Christ—to the glory and praise of God" (Phil. 1:9-11).

"Above all," writes Peter, "love each other deeply." He gives it a practical application: "Offer hospitality to one another without grumbling" (1 Peter 4:8-9). This too is said in the context of "the end of all things is near." Christians are warned that they may experience more opposition and persecution as the return of Christ draws near. Thus this loving support of one another becomes all the more significant.

This is our task as Christians: to serve God by doing his will, bringing the good news of God's love to others in word and deed. To be engaged in the work Jesus has given us to do is the best preparation for his coming.

As he urged his disciples to be ready for his coming, he spoke of the need for a steward to be faithful in carrying out his duties and said, "It will be good for that servant whom the master finds doing so when he returns" (Luke 12:43).

Someone once asked Martin Luther what he would do if he knew Christ would return the next day. He replied, "I would plant a tree"—in other words, he would continue carrying out his normal activities. This is what Paul told the Thessalonians who were inclined to leave their usual occupations and just wait for Christ to appear: continue in your work. This was also his message to the Corinthians. He advised them not to make any changes in their lives, not even to enter marriage or attempt to get out of slavery, but to continue working in the situation in which God had placed them, "for the time is short" (1 Cor. 7:29).

No one knows when Christ will return. Christians are therefore prepared to meet him at any time. The best preparation is to maintain a living relationship of faith in Christ by using the means of grace and continuing in the communion of saints, and to live responsibly, serving our fellow creatures in the vocation God has given us.

11

Why Is It Important?

Why does the Bible give so much attention to the return of Jesus? It is now nearly 2000 years since the words were written, and the event that the New Testament foretells has not yet occurred. Although, as we have seen, it is possible that the fulfillment will come during our lifetime, it is also possible that it may not be for another 2000 years. No one knows. Of what value to us, or to the Christians who have lived and died during these centuries, is all this talk about the second coming?

It can be beneficial to us in several ways.

1. It strengthens our faith by turning our attention to Christ—away from ourselves. All of us tend to think most about ourselves: our problems, our needs and desires, our faith. But the more we focus on ourselves, the less we think about God, and the weaker our relationship to him becomes. The more difficult it becomes, also, to be faithful Christians.

Someone has observed that the middle letter of sin is "I." The central thrust of the Christian message is the inability of human beings to fulfill God's purposes, but the complete sufficiency of Christ to accomplish in and for us all that is good. Thus if our faith is to endure and bear fruit, it is necessary that Christ be at the center of our existence in every way.

To dwell on the return of Christ is one way to keep him in the center. When we think of his coming, we are reminded of what Christ has done—how he has already defeated the enemy, and that in spite of the evil that still troubles us, he is even now the supreme ruler of all. It only remains for him to return and to claim his kingdom. His power, which was exhibited in his resurrection and will be evident again in his return, carries us through this life to share glory with him. But it is only a faith that is anchored in Christ that enables us to reach this goal. "This is the victory that has overcome the world, even our faith" (1 John 5:4). When our life is "hid in Christ," we are "more than conquerors, through him who loved us" (Rom. 8:37).

2. It gives us courage to face trials. The Bible tells us not to be surprised by the difficulties that may come to us in life. On the contrary, it warns us that we may expect our situation as Christians to get worse as time goes on. But it assures us that in the end God's kingdom will be established. This outcome will be accomplished by the triumphant return of Christ, who will subdue every opponent.

In other words, the message of Christ's coming gives hope to people who struggle through the problems and defeats of life. If we didn't have this assurance, we might be tempted to give up the struggle. Or we might be driven to a frenzied effort to overcome the world's evils by ourselves. And this would inevitably lead to despair or cynicism.

But we can endure almost anything if we are sure something better awaits us—if we have hope. This assurance is uppermost in the scriptural descriptions of the second coming. After speaking of the resurrection hope, Paul exhorts the Corinthians, "Therefore, my dear brothers, stand firm. Let nothing move you. Always give yourself fully to the work of the Lord, because you know your labor in the Lord is not in vain" (1 Cor. 15:58). Jesus himself encourages us, "He who stands firm to the end will be saved" (Matt. 10:22).

3. It stirs us to be in constant readiness. Since we do not know when Christ will come, we are to be prepared at any time. "Live as if you knew he would return today" is good Christian advice. John wrote, "Everyone who has this hope in him purifies himself, just as he is pure" (1 John 3:3). Peter said, "The end of all things is near. Therefore be clear minded and self-controlled so that you can pray" (1 Peter 4:7).

Because our human nature is still with us, we are prone to become lazy in our faith. The promise of Christ's return motivates us to greater diligence in using God's gifts to maintain our relationship with him.

The message of the second coming is primarily one of encouragement to Christians. To others it may be a warning of impending judgment—a call to repentance. But to believers it is good news. It strengthens our faith. Christ is coming again! Not to suffer, but to reign. He brings with him blessing and victory for all who are his.

Stand up and lift up your heads because your redemption is drawing near.